I Want A Puppy

2021 Edition

Tristan Pulsifer and

Jacquelyn Elnor Johnson

Crimson Hill
Books

www.CrimsonHillBooks.com

First edition, June 2017.

Second edition, January 2021.

Cataloguing in Publication Data

Pulsifer, Tristan | Johnson, Jacquelyn Elnor

I Want A Puppy | Best Pets For Kids Series

Description: Crimson Hill Books trade hardcover edition | Nova Scotia, Canada

ISBN: 978-1-989595-86-2 (Hardcover – Ingram)

BISAC: JNF003060 Juvenile Nonfiction: Animals - Dogs |
JNF003170 Juvenile Nonfiction: Animals - Pets |
JNF051150 Juvenile Nonfiction: Science & Nature – Zoology

THEMA: WNGD - Dogs as pets |
YNNH1 - Children's / Teenage general interest: Pets & pet care: dogs |
YNNH - Children's / Teenage general interest: Pets & pet care
Record available at https://www.bac-lac.gc.ca/eng/Pages/home.aspx

Cover Photo: Ivonne Wierink, stockfresh.com
Book design: Jesse Johnson

We are pet owners, not veterinarians. Nothing included in this book is meant to serve as medical advice. If you suspect your pet is ill, please see your local vet. We accept no liability concerning your pet ownership.

Crimson Hill Books
(a division of)
Crimson Hill Products Inc.
Wolfville, Nova Scotia
Canada

Contents

Chapter One

What is it like to have a Puppy or a Dog?

This happy pup is enjoying a run at a dog park.

There are one billion pet dogs in the world. That's one dog for every seven people alive today!

This means that millions of families have pet dogs.

Is your family one of them? Or are you reading this book because you really want a puppy or a dog?

If so, this book will tell you more about your puppy or dog, or the one you want, than you know right now.

Here's what you'll find in this book:

- What it's **really** like to have a puppy or dog
- Where to find your new pet
- How to puppy-proof your home
- What your new pet needs to be healthy and happy
- Teaching your puppy good manners
- How to deal with 'bad' dog behaviour, and
- Ideas for what to name your puppy.

What makes dogs so popular as pets?

Almost everywhere in the world, dogs are the most popular pet.

Maybe we love dogs because they're so friendly. Dogs are always excited to see you.

Or it could be because they always want to do whatever you're doing.

Dogs are always ready to play. Or just hang out with you and do whatever you are doing.

And they are just about always happy. Did you know that dogs are the only animal that knows how to smile at people?

Dogs are also the only animal that knows how to 'read' human body language. This includes expressions on people's faces!

If you are happy, or sad, or worried, or afraid, your dog knows it. Dogs understand human emotions.

Some people think that pets look like their owners. What do you think about that?

Another special thing about having a pet dog is they can be good companions. Dogs raised to be pets enjoy being with people.

Dogs also like to be useful. They want to be helpful to people. Long ago, all dogs had jobs helping people. Today, most dogs are pets, though some still perform important jobs.

Dogs have special abilities to hear and smell. This means they can be trained to do jobs people can't do. One of these important jobs dogs do is find people who are lost or buried after an earthquake or avalanche.

Another useful job some dogs do is help police in stopping criminals. Others have been trained to help disabled people live more comfortably.

Some dogs are actors in movies, TV and online. Dogs are natural performers!

These are just a few of the many jobs dogs can do. If you want to know more about working dogs, see the series Dogs With Jobs. You can find it on Netflix.

Dogs are loyal. They won't suddenly decide you aren't their friend. When they like you, they keep on liking you. And they know how to show their affection for people in their family!

What do puppies and dogs need?

Puppies and dogs need all the same things people need – water, food, shelter and friends.

Here's the list of what you need for your puppy or dog:

- Fresh, clean, **cool water** to drink.

- **Healthy food**. Buy puppy chow or dog chow that is designed for their breed, weight and age.

- A **warm, safe home** with their own comfortable **dog bed** for sleeping or getting away to when they need to rest.

Occasionally dogs need good **medical care**. All puppies need shots to prevent serious illnesses. All dogs need to visit the vet once a year for their **annual check-up**.

The person who is a combined doctor, dentist and surgeon for pets is called a veterinarian. (Say this word like this: VET-trin-air-ee-yan). Veterinarians are also sometimes called, "Vets."

Every dog needs **two good walks a day,** including time to run off their leash and socialize with their dog friends. Each walk needs to be at least half an hour to be sure your dog gets enough exercise.

Dogs need **a calm, loving home** where they are treated with kindness and respect; exactly the same thing people need.

Dogs are very much like people in many ways. Scientists have discovered that their brains are surprisingly like our brains. They think a lot like we do when we are about 3 years old.

Dogs feel many of the same emotions people feel, including joy, fear, anger and sadness.

Also like people, they sometimes act badly. Or make mistakes. They might chew on your furniture, or pee (wee) on the rug, or bark when you want to go to sleep. In this book, we will talk about all these 'bad dog' behaviours and how to understand your dog and teach her better manners.

No one really wants to be around a rude, out-of-control or scary dog. They don't want to be around a rude, out-of-control or scary person, either. So, just like kids (and people of all ages) dogs have to learn some manners and what is good behaviour and how to be polite.

Here are some other things you need to be prepared for about puppies and dogs:

1. They shed hair and **need to have their coats brushed**. Dogs with long hair need to be brushed every day.

Dogs left alone too often get lonely.

2. Dogs need **cleaning and grooming**, including baths, cleaning their ears and teeth and clipping the tips of their claws.

3. **Dogs are very unhappy if they are left alone for a long time.** If everyone in your family spends all day in school or at work, having a dog might not be your best choice for a pet. You might be better off choosing a different pet that is content to be left alone a lot of the time.

4. **The bigger the dog, the more they eat** (and poop). That means spending more money on dog food and more work to clean up your yard.

5. If you rent your home, you may need to get permission from the property manager or owner to have a dog.

6. If you live in some cities, you may need to buy a **dog license** in order to have a dog.

7. In some countries there are very strict laws about having pet dogs. Usually, you can find out what the pet laws are for where you live by looking online.

Who wouldn't like having a dog?

If you already have a senior dog or elderly dog, it isn't fair to expect them to put up with a bouncy puppy.

If you have another dog, or cat, you need to introduce a new pet slowly. It may take some time for them to become friends. You can't leave your pets alone together until you are sure they have learned to get along and not fight.

If you are away from home almost all the time, dogs worry about being left alone. And when they need to go, they need to go. It isn't fair to get angry when a dog wets the floor because he couldn't wait for someone to come home and let him outside.

If your family is planning to move, or renovating your home (renovating means making a lot of big changes like building a new garage or a bedroom in the loft) now probably isn't the time to adopt a new pet.

That's also true of getting a new pet during Christmas or other holidays when there's lots going on at your house. There's just too much happening for a new family member to be able to settle in and get used to their new life.

These are all things for you and your family to talk about. If you are going to welcome a puppy or a dog into your family, you want it to be at a happy time when everyone is relaxed. Not stressed.

Summer vacation is an ideal time to add a dog to your family. That's when you can take lots of time to be with your new pet.

Dogs, like people, feel homesick for their former home. They need time to adjust to their new home. They need to get to know you and like you and learn they can trust you.

What dogs like

Dogs are generally easy to please. They mostly like what kids like. Ok, so dogs don't play video games or text their friends or care much about monster trucks or doing skateboard tricks. That isn't important.

What dogs do like is attention. They like a LOT of attention. They don't just like it, they have to have it. If you want to have a dog, you have to be prepared to spend a lot of time with them. They want to be your new best friend. They want you to show them a lot of love!

They like it when you scratch them behind the ears, but don't like it when you pat the top of their head. You probably don't like that either when someone bigger than you does it PLONK-PLONK-PLONK on your head. It kind of hurts.

Dogs playing in a field. Photo: Katrin B, pixabay.com

Dogs like it when there's something interesting going on. Dogs get bored easily, which can lead to trouble.

They like to eat dog food, people food, treats and anything else they can get. Dogs are never fussy eaters, unless they're sick.

Don't leave food out on the counter (work-top) and expect your dog to ignore it!

Just about all dogs love car rides!

They also love going for a swim. And rolling around in stinky stuff. To us, this might be disgusting. To a dog, it's wonderful!

Dogs love running and playing with other dogs. They need their dog friends, too. Just like you need your human friends.

Dogs do a lot of funny things, another great reason to have a dog! They always cheer you up if you've had a hard day.

Like people, dogs have individual personalities. Some are more curious than others. Some are more barky than others. Some are friendlier than others. Some are more shy with strangers than others. Some just want to get on your lap, even if they're way too big to fit!

Part of the fun of adopting a puppy or a dog is getting to know who they really are.

There are purebred dogs and mixed breed dogs. With all dogs, if you have a chance to meet their parents, you will have a fairly good idea of who that dog will turn out to be.

Some breeds are known for certain behaviours. For example, German Shepherds always want to be guard dogs. They might try to 'guard' your home from strangers who come to visit. They need to learn to welcome your guests.

Dogs that were originally bred to herd sheep can't seem to forget this. They try to herd people, nosing them or pushing them where the dog wants the person to go. This can be a problem if you have a really young brother or sister who is just learning to walk. A big dog could knock them down.

13

Little children also need to learn to be kind to dogs, and not pull their ears or their tails or try to sit on top of them.

Dogs trained to be hunters will try to hunt and kill small wild animals. Then they bring what they killed back to you, as a 'prize.' You may not like them doing this every time they get off their leash!

Mixed breed dogs are usually more easy-going than purebred dogs. Mixed breed dogs don't have some of the health problems that purebreds are known for.

Many Dalmatians are deaf (this means they can't hear anything). Most dachshunds have back problems. Labrador Retrievers, the most popular dog breed in United States, Canada, Australia and New Zealand, easily become too fat if their owners aren't careful.

Pugs and all dogs with short noses and flat faces have breathing problems.

Before you become a pet owner, you need to be aware of what the problems can be for the type of pet you choose. If you choose a purebred dog, you should know that you may have higher vet bills than with a mixed breed dog.

Reading this book is a good start on everything you need to know to be a good pet parent. When you truly care about your pet and do what is best for her, what you get will be a happy, healthy and well-behaved dog who is your best friend!

This Labrador Retriever puppy is five months old.

Chapter Two

All About Puppies

A Golden Retriever dam with her pups.

A mother dog is called a dam. The father is a sire.

Mother dogs are pregnant for about 65 days, or just a bit longer than two months. Then they give birth to their pups. They might have only one puppy or up to as many as eight. The most puppies a dam ever had at one time was 17!

Smaller dams have only one or two pups, while bigger breed dams usually have a larger litter (litter means

This tiny pup is just a few days old.

all the puppy brothers and sisters born at the same time).

Puppies are born blind, deaf (this means they can't see or hear) and completely helpless. Right after they are born, their dam licks them to get their breathing working properly. Then she gently nudges them towards her body to get their first meal of dog milk. It is their perfect food.

Newborn puppies are so tiny you could easily hold one in your hand. They spend almost all their time sleeping because they are growing so fast. They stay close to their dam and litter mates for warmth. Just like children, dogs need good sleep to grow quickly.

17

When puppies are about three weeks old, they open their eyes for the first time. This is also when their hearing gets better and their baby teeth start to grow in.

When they are between two weeks and five weeks old puppies start to walk.

At first they are very awkward. But soon they are running around. They especially love to play hide-and-seek. It's fun to give them puppy toys and see what they do next. Puppies are very curious and are always learning.

They do lots of play fighting with their brothers and sisters. This is how they start to learn about how to behave in a dog family, which is called a pack.

At the same time they are learning about how to behave in a people family from you and your family.

Their mother, the dam, will push them away when it is time for them to learn how to eat and drink from their food dishes. She will show them how to do this.

If the dam and her puppies are outdoor dogs or feral (wild) dogs, she will teach her puppies how to avoid danger, find safe shelter and hunt for food.

A wild dam will also protect her puppies from harm until they are big enough to protect themselves.

All dams are good mothers. They teach their puppies everything they need to know about how to stay healthy, warm and safe.

Even female dogs who have never had their own puppies can be good mothers to orphan animals.

Orphan means they have lost their parents. There are many stories about dogs who 'adopt' baby animals and treat them as their own until they are adults.

All puppies need to be touched and held by people to grow up to be good pets. They must have a chance to get used to people and learn to trust that people will be gentle and kind to them.

Very tiny puppies also need to learn where to go to the toilet. At first, they are much too small to go outside. They need to be shown that the place to go is on the newspapers spread out on the floor.

When they get a bit bigger, puppies need to go outside once every hour. They are so small that they can't wait longer than this. This is one of the reasons that it is more work to have a puppy than a dog who already knows what part of the yard she is allowed to use as her toilet.

Puppies are old enough to leave their mother when they can find their own food and no longer need her milk to survive. The longer puppies can stay with their dam, the more they learn about being good pets.

Puppies need to be at least two months old to be old enough to leave their mother and litter-mates and adjust to their new home. For some breeds, staying with their mother for at least three months is better.

When puppies are about four months old, they lose their baby teeth. That's when their adult teeth grow in. They chew on everything in sight to ease the pain of these new teeth coming in. To help them, give them small ice cubes. They will try to chew these and the coldness will soothe their sore gums.

This is a Saint Bernard puppy. She's two months old.

Puppies grow into adult dogs when they are about one year old. By then, they are old enough to become parents and have their own puppies. However, your vet will recommend that your dog gets neutered before then. This is having a small operation. It is a bit uncomfortable for your dog, but they soon forget about that.

Being neutered means that your dog will not ever have puppies. Dogs that are neutered usually live healthier and longer lives.

When puppies play with their litter-mates, they nip each other. This is just normal play for puppies. Puppies have sharp little teeth, but usually a bite doesn't really hurt.

If your puppy nips you while playing, pretend that it really hurt and say "Ouch!" loudly. They will understand.

Here's why. When puppies are playing together, if one of them yelps it means someone else nipped too hard. The yelp is the signal to stop doing that! When you do the same, your puppy will learn it's not Ok and stop nipping.

When a puppy is old enough to leave his dam, he is old enough to start learning puppy manners like going outside, not nipping people and simple commands like "Come!" "Sit!" and "Stay!"

The way to teach puppies is to reward them with praise and treats when they do something right, even if it is just a little bit right.

When they do something wrong, ignore them.

Puppies are smart and quickly learn how to please you and get their reward. Use puppy treats or tiny pieces of raw, peeled carrot as training treats.

Hold a puppy with both hands. This is a Border Collie puppy.

<u>Chapter Three</u>

All About Dogs

This is a Bernese Mountain dog. They were originally bred to rescue people.

Dogs first appeared on earth about 40 million years ago. But it is only for about the last 30,000 years or so that dogs and people have lived together.

For a very long time, dogs wanted to live near people, but not with people. Dogs liked living near people because people threw out tasty scraps of meat. Dogs liked getting free dinners.

People liked having the dogs nearby. This was because dogs scared off other dangerous animals that might attack.

Gradually, people took the gentlest puppies and taught them to be guard dogs.

Then people learned that dogs could help with other jobs, like carrying supplies or hauling in fishing nets. Dogs were good, strong workers who didn't ask for much. Dogs and people began to rely on each other.

People discovered that dogs can be really smart. Just as people changed dogs and how they live, dogs have changed people and our lives.

Even though, very long ago, both dogs and wolves had the same ancient ancestor, modern dogs aren't wolves.

Dogs also aren't people, even though some owners like to treat their dogs like people.

Dogs are still very much like wolves; but they are also very much like people. They are still able to live in the wild world, as wild wolf-dogs. But dogs have also learned how to live in the tame world with people as our pets.

What do pet dogs eat?

Some owners make their dog food. If you are interested in doing this, there are recipes online. But doing this takes time. Most people prefer to buy dog food that is already made at the grocery store. It can be dry food (it comes in paper bags) or wet dog food (it comes in cans or plastic containers).

When you buy a quality dog food, it is specially made to have all the right nutrition for your dog. Dogs don't need to eat people food to be healthy.

While dog food is best for dogs, they can have a little bit of people food for a treat. Cooked white rice or pasta and cooked lean meat are safe for dogs to eat.

They can also eat these for a treat: apple, orange, watermelon, carrot sticks, green beans, cucumber, zucchini or baked potato. Any fruit or vegetables you give your dog needs to be carefully washed and peeled, with no core, rind or seeds.

How many different breeds of dogs are there?

There are more than 400 recognized dog breeds. Some breeds are ones you probably already know, like German Shepherds and Labrador Retrievers. Others, like Lapphunds, are rare.

How big do dogs get?

The range of sizes a dog can be is truly amazing! The largest breeds of dogs are Great Danes, English Mastiffs, Newfoundland dogs, Saint Bernards and Leonbergers.

The heaviest dog ever known is Aicama Zorba, an English Mastiff who weighs 342 pounds (155 kg).

The biggest dog was Giant George, who lived in Arizona. He was a Great Dane who was 7 feet 3 inches (2.2 meters) tall when he stood up on his hind legs! He ate 180 pounds (82 kg) of food every month!

How small can dogs be?

If you want a small dog, these are the breeds to consider:

- Chihuahua.
- Toy or Miniature Poodle.
- Shih Tzu.
- Miniature Schnauzer.
- Maltese.
- Bichon Frise.
- Lhasa Apso.
- Norwich Terrier.
- Chinese Crested.

The smallest known dog is Boo Boo, a long-haired female Chihuahua. She is just 4 inches (10 cm) tall and weighs just 2 pounds (.9 kg). She is so tiny she can fit in a teacup!

How long do dogs live?

With good care, pet dogs live, on average, eight to 15 years.

Wild dogs have much shorter lives than that.

Usually, the smaller breeds live longer than big dogs.

Why do dogs bark? Why do they howl?

There are as many different reasons for dogs barking as there are for people talking.

An interesting thing is that wild dogs and wolves hardly ever bark. It seems that barking is something dogs developed to communicate with people. (Cats did the same thing with meowing and purring).

Dogs bark to tell us they're excited, afraid, or because they want something. They also bark when they're bored and when they are protecting their home and people.

Dogs howl to say, "I'm over here. Where are you?" to other dogs. They may also howl when they are in distress. This means something is very wrong for them right now and they need you to do something about it.

Dogs who have not learned how to be home alone will howl to get someone to come and look after them. They can learn not to do this, but it takes time and patience.

Do dogs have pawprints like people have fingerprints?

For people, fingerprints are unique. This means that your fingerprints are like no one else's.

Dog paw prints aren't unique. All we can tell is that the paw print belonged to a dog, rather than another animal, such as a fox or cat.

But, surprisingly, every dog DOES have something completely unique to him or her. It's their nose print!

The Canadian Kennel Club was the first in the world to recognize this and register members by their nose-prints. This is now done by kennel clubs (they register dog breeds) everywhere.

What plants, plant foods or people food are poisons for dogs?

The safest thing for dogs to eat is a good brand of dog food. Many things are dangerous for dogs, including pork chop bones (they can shatter and injure your dog), candy, milk or ice cream (it makes dogs sick) and all of these things:

- **Poinsettias** (say this word like this: Poy-n-set-taz). Poinsettias are the plants with big red leaves that we often see around Christmas-time. Though they are beautiful, chewing on poinsettias can be deadly for pets.

- **Marijuana** (say this word like this: Mare-i-wahn-a)

- **Mistletoe** (say this word like this: MISS-ill-toe)

Other people food that is poisonous for dogs:

- **Chewing gum** or anything with Xylitol in it. Xylitol is a chemical in sugarless gum, many types of **candy** and also in toothpaste.

- Wine, beer or **anything with alcohol** in it.

- **Avocados**, **onions** and **garlic** are poisons for dogs. So are **grapes** and **raisins**.

- Anything with **caffeine** in it will make your dog sick. There is caffeine in coffee, tea, soda, hot chocolate and chocolate bars.

- Don't give any **dairy product** to dogs because it will make them sick. Dairy products are milk, cheese and ice cream.

- **Macadamia nuts** are bad for dogs. Just six can make a dog very sick.

- Never give your puppy or dog **raw eggs, meat or fish**. They can't have the fat trimmed from meat, either cooked or raw. All of these will make them ill.

- There is **cyanide** in the pits of peaches, plums and persimmons. Cyanide is a deadly poison.

- Eating **anything with salt, sugar**, and anything with **yeast** in it (like bread dough) causes a bellyache for your dog.

Here are some other things you might have in your home or your garage, yard or garden that are dangerous for dogs to eat:

- **Medicines meant for people**, especially aspirin or acetaminophen. Never give people medicine to pets unless your veterinarian recommends it. If your pet does accidently swallow any medicine, especially pills for coughs and colds, diet pills, or any pain pills, call your vet right away!

- **Vitamins and supplements** meant for people can harm your pets.

- **Tap water** has added chemicals and bleach in it. This is healthy for people, but not for dogs. Give pets spring water or bottled water. Or pour out their drinking water and let it stand in an uncovered dish overnight (where your pets can't get it). The chemicals and bleach will mostly evaporate into the air, leaving the water safe to give to your pets.

- **Antifreeze** is good in cars, but deadly for pets. It needs to be kept in bottles with tight lids.

- **Bleach** is useful for cleaning but also deadly for pets. **Moth balls** (used to prevent moths from chewing holes in towels, sheets and blankets) look like toys to a dog, but they are also a dangerous poison for them.

- **Other poisons used in the garden** – weed-killer, rodent killer, mosquito and bug repellant – all are dangerous for pets.

Just like human children, pets need to be protected from harm.

Can dogs see in colour?

When we say a person is "colour blind," what we mean is that they see colours, but don't see bright green and red. For them, greens and reds are mostly gray or brownish-gray. This is close to the way dogs see the world.

Dogs love car rides. This Pug is enjoying the ride!

If you were a dog, everything would be dark blue, light blue, gray, light yellow, darker yellow-brown and very dark gray.

Things that most people see as red or bright green would be grayish-brown.

But dogs see much better than people can when it is early morning, or almost dark out. They have very good vision at night. However, like people, dogs can't see anything when it is totally dark.

Can dogs hear better than people?

Puppies and dogs can hear things people can't hear. Some sounds that aren't too loud for us are actually painfully loud to dogs.

31

How well can dogs smell or taste things?

Dogs have a sense of smell that is so much better than what people have we can only imagine what it would be like to have a dog's sniffing abilities!

Imagine you are out walking your dog and she sees a friend also walking their dog. While you stop to chat, the dogs are chatting, too. But they don't use words, or barking. They use their sense of smell and dog body language.

The first thing dogs do to greet each other is sniff their faces, then their rears. This seems very rude to people! But to dogs, what they are doing is gathering information.

What have you been doing today? Where did you go? Who did you see? Did you have something nice to eat? Are you well?

These are all the kinds of things you and your friend might talk about. They're also all the things one dog can learn from another, just by sniffing!

How to understand 'dog talk'

Dogs use body language to communicate, just like people do. You will quickly learn what your dog is trying to tell you!

When a dog's tail is up in the air and their mouth is open, they are happy.

When they have their tail between their legs and are looking down, they are worried that they're in trouble.

When they show their teeth, flatten their ears and growl, they are feeling threatened. They could be about to bite!

When they look directly at you, they are looking for instructions about what to do next. Or not do.

Why do dogs wag their tails?

Another way dogs tell you what's important in their world is with their tails.

When their tail is high and wagging, they are excited or possibly annoyed.

Wagging their tail low and very fast means they are afraid of something.

A tail that is in the middle and wagging means a happy dog.

What about a tail that is only wagging in one direction? Here's what this means. Wagging towards the dog's left side means, "I'm a bit worried." Wagging to the right means, "I'm happy!"

Do dogs understand people?

It is true that dogs understand body language that people use. Body language is things like frowning, smiling and touching. But do dogs also understand people talk?

They do. Dogs are able to learn many words, including their own names and the names of things in their world.

Scientists used to think that dogs could learn about 35

words, or maybe as many as 50 words for a very smart dog.

This turns out not to be true. When dogs have an opportunity to learn new words they can learn a LOT more than this! Dogs can learn hundreds of words if you teach them the words for things. You could start by teaching them the names of their toys.

Some breeds learn much faster than others. Labrador Retrievers, German Shepherds, Standard Poodles, Border Collies and Sheepdogs are known as especially smart breeds of dogs.

Why do dogs bite?

Dogs bite when they feel threatened. This means they think someone is going to hurt them. They use biting to defend themselves.

If you have a dog biting problem, you can teach your dog not to bite. While he or she is learning this you will need to put a muzzle on your dog when you go out for a walk. A muzzle is just a strap on their snout that prevents a dog from being able to bite anyone.

Can people get sick from their dogs?

Yes. Some people are allergic to dogs. Being near a dog means they cough, get itchy skin or a rash.

Some dogs have no hair or less hair or curly hair. People with a dog allergy can usually have these types of dogs and not have their allergy problems. These breeds are:

- **Curly haired dogs** such as Irish Water Spaniels, Poodles and Portuguese Water Dogs

- **Hairless dogs**. Hairless Terriers, Chinese Crested Dogs

- **Low-shedding dogs**. Basenjis, Chihuahuas, Greyhounds and Maltese dogs.

- **Terriers**. Kelly Blue Terriers, Schnauzers and Wheaten Terriers.

There are some illnesses that people can catch from dogs, including a cold and some more serious diseases, such as Lyme disease, ringworm and rabies.

Always wash your hands before and after you touch your dog. Don't allow your dog to give you dog kisses or lick your face. Doing this will help keep you and your pet healthy.

Can cats and dogs be friends?

Yes they can.

Cats and dogs can learn to get along well together. Dogs can also learn to be friends with other pets, such as bearded dragons.

Some small pets are very frightened of dogs. If you have a hamster or guinea pig, keep them away from your dog.

There can be problems when you already have one pet, and then suddenly there is a new pet in your home. Your 'old' pet might be jealous. Or he or she might worry that there won't be enough food.

Pets have to meet each other and get to know each other gradually. Never leave pets alone together until you are sure they are friends.

A girl with her puppy. Photo: Pisauikan, pixabay.com

Can dogs love people as much as people love dogs?

People have been asking this question for a very long time. Only recently do we have the answer.

It's the answer most dog owners were hoping for. Yes, dogs can love people, and now we have proof! When dogs and people they care about are together, they both release oxytocin (say it like this: OX-ee-toe-sin) in their brains.

Oxytocin is a hormone. Hormones are natural chemicals in the body. They are released by emotions and help cause them. Oxytocin is called the "love hormone" because people – and dogs – in love have more oxytocin.

Chapter Four

How And Where To Get Your Puppy Or Dog

Do you think black dogs are lucky? This black dog is hoping you do!

With so many to choose from, how can you pick out the right puppy or dog for you and your family?

Always choose the pet that is curious, playful and friendly. They need to be clean, with bright eyes, a pink mouth and gums, a cool nose and clean ears. All these are signs of excellent health.

You need to decide: do you want a puppy or an adult dog? Remember that puppies are lots of fun, but they need more time and care.

Puppies might need more visits to the vet.

Adult dogs already show their true personality – whether they are shy or very friendly and whether they mostly want to run around and have lots of energy or they are content to enjoy quiet times at home.

Every dog, just like every person, has their own character and quirks.

When you get a puppy, getting to know who they are is part of the fun.

When you get an adult dog, they already have their adult personality. They may also have some bad behaviour and find it hard to change to please you. This is especially true if you adopt a dog who had careless or cruel owners. It may be hard for them to learn to trust you. But the good news is, they can if you are gentle and patient.

It isn't fair to any pet to get him and then decide you don't really like him very much. When you adopt a pet, you are making a promise that you will always give this animal everything they need to be healthy and happy for their entire life.

They are joining your family.

Make sure you choose the puppy or dog that you can make this promise to. Keep your promise!

This mixed breed dog is at the pet shelter. He hopes you'll come and take him home.

Where to find your new pet

Maybe you have a family member or friend who has a dog they want to find a good new home for. Or their dam just had babies and they give you a puppy.

Or you could look at the free online ads for your area. Often, someone is looking for good homes for puppies.

Another place to look is at pet rescue shelters. Some will have all kinds of pets available. Others specialize in finding new homes for only certain breeds of puppies and dogs. A big advantage of adopting your new pet from a pet rescue shelter is you know you are getting a pet that is healthy.

When you adopt a rescue or shelter dog, you also know that you are saving their life. This is important, because there are always more pets that need a good home than there are families to adopt them.

Your adopted dog will have had all their shots and have been checked by a vet to be sure they are ready to find their forever home. Pets from shelters also have a tattoo in their ear or a microchip. This helps them get home if they are ever lost.

Most dogs that you find at rescue shelters are mixed breed dogs, though they sometimes also have a purebred dog available.

Reasons to choose a particular breed of dog are that you like the way they look, their size, their personality or there is something else special about them.

If you want a special breed of dog, then you might go to a dog breeder. They are in the business of raising and selling healthy puppies. Be very careful if you do this. Only consider dogs that have been hand-raised inside a clean, loving home.

Bad breeders raise dogs and keep them outside or in barns inside cages. These dogs usually do not get enough to eat or any shots or medical care. Their cages are dirty. These breeders run what is called "puppy mills."

Owners who run puppy mills abuse their dogs, which is against the law in most places. If you visit a breeder who you suspect is really running a puppy mill, the right thing to do is report them to animal control authorities or police.

What are the most popular dog breeds?

Some popular dog breeds are:

- Dachshund

- Labrador Retriever

- Newfoundland (Newfie)

- Pekinese

- Dalmatian

- Irish Setter

- Collie

- Jack Russell Terrier

- Bull Terrier

There are many more breeds of dogs. They come in all shapes and sizes! If you want to know more about what different breeds there are, a good place to learn is at dog shows.

This is also the place to talk to dog breeders, if you decide you want a purebred puppy. These shows take place a few times a year in major cities. You can find them advertised online.

How to choose your puppy

Be sure the puppy or dog you adopt is healthy. This is always true when you adopt from a shelter that is a registered charity, such as the Humane Society or SPCA. When you are given your new pet, or find them online, the first thing you will need to do is take them to the vet for a full check-up and shots.

This is a Finnish Lapphund puppy. They're a rare breed.

Also, unless you intend to breed your dog, you need him or her to be neutered. Neutered means they have a small operation to make sure they never have puppies or cause a female dog to have puppies.

Dogs that are neutered (or spayed) usually are healthier and live longer than if they are allowed to have puppies. There isn't a lot of difference between female dogs and males after they are neutered. The operation means they might be a bit uncomfortable for a few days, but they soon forget about it.

Responsible pet owners make sure to have their pets neutered. They don't let their pets add to the problem of far too many homeless dogs in the world.

This Collie wants to know if you've got any treats?

Remember that a puppy allowed to stay with his or her mother and litter-mates for longer is more socialized. This means more able to be a good pet. A puppy taken from his dam too soon is going to need more help from you to learn to be a good pet.

Don't choose an animal that has runny eyes, a runny nose, dirty ears, a cough or a dull coat. Don't take a pet home just because you feel sorry for him or her. If you do, they might need several visits to the vet. This could be expensive and they still might not survive. Choose a dog that is healthy and happy – they make the best pets.

If you live in United States or Canada, consider adopting a dog with a black coat. Because many North Americans believe black pets are unlucky, often black pups and dogs are the last ones to find a home. This is unfair, because black pets can be just as wonderful (and lucky!) as any other colour.

You might also consider adopting a senior dog. While lots of people want puppies and very young dogs, it is harder for deserving middle-aged or older dogs to find a loving home.

Senior dogs are usually more settled and better-behaved. They have learned all their manners. They can make excellent pets.

Where shouldn't you get your puppy or dog?

Puppies and dogs in pet stores look just as cute as every other puppy or dog. But sometimes, this isn't the best place to find a healthy pet.

The reason is some pet stores get their animals from puppy mills.

What's the best breed of dog to get?

This is a difficult question that only you and your family can answer.

Start by having a conversation about what "best" means for you.

If you live in an apartment or a small home, best might mean you want a small dog that isn't a barker. You don't want to disturb the neighbours! You also need a dog that doesn't need a back yard to run around in, is friendly and easy to train.

Some good choices for apartment or small home families are French Bulldogs, Corgis, Pugs and Poodles.

If you'd love to have a large dog and have lots of space for him, consider a Great Dane, Greyhound or Mastiff. Great Danes are calm and quiet and easy to train. Greyhounds are gentle, playful and like having a yard to run in. Mastiffs are gentle and friendly and known to be really good with younger children. So are Collies.

If you want a livelier dog with lots of personality, you probably want a mid-sized dog like a Dachshund, Beagle or Terrier.

Golden Retrievers, Labrador Retrievers, German Shepherds and Collies are very popular breeds because they are easy to train and they especially like children.

By now, you probably have a good idea of what sort of dog you are going to get. But wait! Before you go ahead and adopt a pet, you need to get their new home ready to welcome them.

Just like any new member to your family, they want to be comfortable and well cared for, so they can quickly feel right at home!

This kind of dog is called a labradoodle. Photo: Skeeze, pixabay.com

<u>Chapter Five</u>

Getting Ready For Your New Pet

These are Springer Spaniels.

If you have younger brothers or sisters, you already know that parents must make their homes safe for children. Good parents put cleaning products away where children can't reach them. They put covers on electrical outlets (power points). They pack away things that could break easily and hurt a baby or child, like glass ornaments.

Puppies need soft toys to chew on, especially when they're teething.

They also need to get rid of anything with small pieces that a baby could put in her mouth. Sometimes, toys that are completely safe for older kids are very dangerous to babies and toddlers. If you have younger brothers and sisters, you probably already know there are some of your things you can't let them play with.

Good pet parents also have to make changes so their homes are safe for their pets.

What do you need to do to make your home puppy-safe, or safe for your new pet dog?

Do this to puppy-proof, or dog-proof, your home

Puppies and dogs run and jump a lot. They can easily knock things over, like empty glasses or lamps. Be sure that there are no heavy things that could fall on top of them and hurt them. Or fall on the floor and break.

All medicines need to be put away. Dogs are curious and if something looks interesting or smells interesting, they could try to eat it.

Some dogs (like all the hounds) will try to eat anything! You could try training them not to do this. It is better to put things they shouldn't ever eat where they can't ever get them.

Make sure there are no string, ribbon, rubber bands or bread bag plastic tabs left out. Also no toys with small pieces, like Lego. Dogs could try to swallow these and choke.

Be careful that there are no lamp or computer chords, or chords from window blinds or curtains that your dog could get tangled in.

Keep tight lids on your recycling, compost and garbage cans that are in the house. Some dogs are terrible garbage hounds!

Houseplants need to be out of reach. Many are poisonous to puppies or dogs.

If your home has a fireplace, keep the fire screen closed. Check that screens on windows are secure.

If your family likes to decorate your home for holidays, be sure that the decorations are out of reach for your pets. Dogs think Christmas tree ornaments are more toys. But the glass balls can easily break into dangerously sharp pieces.

When is a good time to adopt a new pet?

Some people think it is a good idea to give their family a new pet at Christmas time or other big holidays.

But here is something to think about. During the holidays, there's usually lots of rushing around and lots of excitement in the air. Pets can be stressed by all this craziness.

Dogs are surprisingly sensitive. It is easy to laugh at them when they are afraid of things, like the vacuum cleaner, but this is unkind. Try to understand that they truly are frightened. Calm their fears.

To adjust happily to a new home, a pet needs calm, quiet and a routine. He or she needs to have a chance to get comfortable and used to the new house rules. But during holidays, with all the strange smells of holiday foods, different people coming and going and other activities of the season, pets can be very stressed. All these strange smells and sounds can overwhelm them.

At first, when they come into your home, a new pet puppy or dog needs to be in just one room, along with their food dish, water dish, pet bed and some toys. If possible, they should also have something from their former home, like a favourite toy or their blanket. They will be soothed by the familiar smells of that blanket or toy.

A Hungarian Pointer learning walking manners at dog obiedience school. Photo: Katrin B, pixabay.com

Leave the door open and allow them to come out and explore the rest of the house when they are ready.

Dogs need their own dog bed. This can be one you buy at the pet store or online, or you can make a dog bed with a cardboard box and an old blanket or a big cushion in it.

Every dog needs a warm, secure place that is quiet to rest, get away from everyone else and relax or sleep.

If you already have other pets, introduce them gradually.

Dogs are territorial. This means they think they own the area they live in. They will fight other dogs or cats if they feel threatened or think someone might steal their food.

When dogs are wild, they live in groups called packs. Packs hunt together. Everyone in a pack knows who is the top dog, and who everyone else is. When pets live with people, the people are their pack. One of those people is the top dog.

A puppy or dog that you adopt will think that it is scary to leave the home they know, and possibly also their mother, brothers and sisters, to come to your house. At first, you and your home will smell strange to them (and remember, dogs have a MUCH better sense of smell that people do).

A new pet may cry at first. This is just them being frightened and homesick. They will soon get used to their new home if you are kind, gentle and patient.

What is the best time to get a new pet?

Bring a new pet into your life in a calm, happy time for your family.

Not right after a pet you loved has just died. This is a sad time. It isn't fair to a new animal to treat him like just a replacement for the friend you have lost. Give yourself some time to mourn and, eventually, you will be ready to welcome a new pet.

So when is the best time to get a pet? The answer is when you have the time to give him or her lots of care and attention. A time when you will not be rushing around, or stressed for some other reason, because animals are very good at 'reading' people's emotions and feelings.

A nervous home makes nervous pets. A quiet, calm home makes happier, better-behaved and healthier pets. And people.

What do you need to get for your puppy, or dog?

1. **A pet bed.** Dogs love sleeping anywhere that is warm and soft and feels safe. Just be sure that the pet bed you choose is easy for them to get into and out of.

2. **Pet food and water bowls.** These don't need to be fancy, but they should be sturdy and able to go in the dishwasher or easy to clean. You'll need to clean these bowls every day. There should always be fresh, cool water for your puppy or dog to drink. Larger breeds need their food and water bowl to be off the floor, perhaps on a little bench or stool. This is because it is hard for them to bend their head down to eat and swallow. They could easily choke. Smaller breeds of dogs are fine when their food bowl and water bowl are on the floor. Always put the bowls in a quieter corner of the kitchen or nearby, not right in the middle of where everyone is walking.

3. **Puppies need puppy food,** because they are still growing. Buy a good quality dog food if they are older than eight months.

4. **A comfortable collar** and **a leash** for walks.

5. **Dog tags** attached to the collar with your phone number, in case your dog ever gets lost.

6. **Grooming brushes**. Pick the right type for your breed of dog. If you're unsure, ask for advice at a pet store or from your vet.

7. **Dog nail trimmers.**

8. **Toys**. Dogs love balls, chew toys, rubber chew toys and soft toys they are allowed to chew on. They also like frisbees.

9. **A dog crate**. You need this for trips to the vet or if your dog ever travels on a plane. It needs to be big enough for your dog to stand up and turn around, but not larger than that.

10. **Dog treats.** There are lots of different flavours – beef, chicken, tuna and salmon are some you'll see at the grocery store or pet shop.

11. **Training**. Puppies need to go to Puppy School to learn basic commands like "Sit!" "Go to your bed!" and "Give" when they have something that is yours. Puppies graduate to Obedience Training. Some go on from there to learn tricks in Agility Training classes. Dogs love to learn and love to show off what they know. Part of the fun of having a dog is teaching them manners, commands and other cool things they can do.

Dogs don't need much...but they do need what all people need. Fresh air to breathe, clean water, healthy food, warmth, shelter and protection from harm and a good home.

When they are sick, they need medical care from a vet and they may need dog medicine. The thing they need most is your loving kindness and friendship.

Chapter Six

Good Care For Puppies And Dogs

Four Labrador Retriever puppies from the same litter.

One of the first things you need to know about puppies and dogs is how to pick them up. Do this wrong and they could be hurt. Or they could scratch and hurt you.

They wouldn't mean to do this. It is just their instinct to protect themselves.

Here's how to safely pick up a puppy or a dog

Put one hand firmly under their bottom and the other under their chest. Hold the puppy close to your body. Be careful, because a squirmy puppy will try to get away and could easily fall.

It's better to sit on the floor to play with puppies, or on your bed.

Things to never do with your dog

Never do this:

- Pick them up by their tail, the skin behind their neck, or their paw or a leg.

- Let them chew on electrical cords.

- Hit them or kick them.

- Yell at them.

- Throw things at them. They don't understand this. All they learn is to be afraid of you.

- Shout and chase them when they take something that isn't theirs. They will just run away, because they think this is a game you are playing. Or they will be afraid they are in trouble.

- Tease them. This is bullying.

Ears, Teeth, Claws and Fur

Dogs need their teeth cleaned to prevent tooth decay. Do this with a toothbrush and special pet toothpaste. Don't use toothpaste meant for people. It has a chemical in it called Xilitol that is poison for dogs. You could also use a clean, soft cloth that is dampened in warm water to gently clean your dog's teeth.

Dogs usually don't like this. You may need help holding them firmly and holding their mouth open.

Unfortunately, you can't tell them this is so they won't have teeth that hurt. Try to be as gentle and fast at the tooth cleaning as possible.

You could also buy them chews that help keep their teeth clean and healthy.

You need to clean their ears. The soft cloth that is just a bit wet with warm water works for this. Never use a cotton-tip stick.

A cotton ball or soft face cloth dipped in warm water is good for cleaning their ears, nose, around their eyes, their face and under their chin.

How to give a dog a bath

If a dog trembles during a bath, it is very frightened. Be gentle. Don't fill the bathtub. Just put in enough water up to go up to the middle of their legs.

Use dog shampoo. People shampoo is not good for their coat. Make the bath as fast as possible.

Afterwards, wrap them in a warm towel and praise them for being a good dog.

Never spray a dog with perfume, room freshener or a cleaning product. They could try to lick it off and be poisoned!

Your vet can show you how to trim your dog's nails.

All dogs need to be brushed. For long-hair dogs, this is once or twice a day. Short-hair dogs only need to be brushed once or twice a week.

Brush gently, starting with their head and working towards their tail. Some dogs really enjoy being brushed, but others just don't like it. If your dog objects to the brushing, just do it for a minute or so, then finish the job later.

Dogs need their claws trimmed, just like you need your fingernails and toenails trimmed from time to time. If your dog's nails click on the floor, they are too long and need to be clipped.

Your vet can show you how to clip your dog's nails.

Getting good care at the vet.

Signs you need to go to the vet

When puppies have their teeth, face, eyes and ears cleaned the way we have just told you about, they get used to it. They may not enjoy it, but they put up with it because they know you will be gentle.

How to take your dog to the vet

Some dogs are good during car rides. Others bounce around, which could be dangerous for the people in the car, especially the driver. If you have a dog that can't behave in the car, they need to ride in their crate.

Some pets are very afraid of visits to the vet. There are other animals there, strange sounds, strange smells and they just want to go home. If this is your

Dogs need playtime with their dog friends.

dog, it might be best to wait in the car until it is time to meet the vet in the examination room.

When does your dog need to see the vet?

When you first get your pet, take them to meet the vet and have a general examination to be sure they are healthy and have had all their shots.

It's also your chance to ask questions about good pet care.

You need to call the vet if:

- Your puppy or dog stops eating, seems to have no energy and sleeps a lot.

- Your dog can't stop throwing up or can't poop or pee.

- Your dog's personality changes suddenly.

- Call immediately if your dog swallows something that is poison for them, like chocolate, mistletoe or poinsettias.

- A dog that is bleeding and it won't stop, has breathing problems or has been hit by a car needs the vet immediately.

Keep your vet's number near the phone or where you can get it quickly. Call them and ask what to do. They will probably tell you to come to their office.

How to give a pill to a dog

Sometimes, the vet will send you home with medicine to give your dog. Your vet will show you how to do this, but here's a reminder.

- Gently open your dog's mouth (but not too wide).

- Flip the pill to the back of his mouth.

- Gently hold his jaws closed while holding his head as if he was looking up at you.

- Lightly stroke his neck until he swallows.

- Check his mouth to make sure the pill went down and isn't hidden under his tongue.

What about fleas and ticks?

A dog that scratches a lot might have fleas. Look very closely at her coat, parting the fur to see the skin. If there are tiny black specks, she has fleas. Buy a flea collar. If this doesn't get rid of the fleas, your vet can help.

Ticks are worse than fleas because ticks can carry diseases. Dogs that are outside, especially in places with tall grass or lots of trees can easily get ticks. The ticks mostly go to places near the dog's ears, head, neck and shoulders.

When your dog comes in from outside, you need to check carefully for ticks. Remove them with tweezers, not your fingers because this could spread disease. If your dog has been bitten by a tick, remove the tick and then call your vet for advice.

Senior dogs

If you adopt (or you have) a senior dog, you might have noticed that their behaviour changes when they get older.

Many senior dogs become less energetic. They might not want to go as far on walks, because they have painful joints. They walk more slowly.

They might sleep more. And snore.

They might change in what they like to eat.

All of this is normal for a senior dog. Just like many older people, they want an easy life.

How to help an overweight dog

It is estimated that half of all the pet dogs in Britain and United States are overweight! This might be because they ate too many treats, didn't get enough exercise, or have an illness that causes obesity.

(Obesity is the term doctors and vets use when a person or a pet is very overweight).

Sadly, obese dogs don't live as long and aren't as healthy as they would if their weight was normal.

Don't let your pet have cookies (biscuits), chips (crisps) or other people snacks. They can't have bread, gravy or dripping from the pan after meat is cooked, ice cream, candies (sweets), gum or canned meats meant for humans. The only thing that is healthy for dogs to eat is a quality brand of dog food or food you make for them from a dog food recipe.

Switch your overweight dog to wet food (soft dog food). It's higher in protein and has less carbs than dry food. Cut out all dog treats except bits of carrot or apple slices.

You should take your dog to the vet and ask for her advice before putting your pet on a weight-loss diet. It might be that your dog has an illness that is causing the extra weight.

This is a pitbull. They are a breed that is banned in some places because people breed pitbulls to be attack-dogs. They aren't bad dogs. People made them act this way. With loving kindness almost any dog can be a good pet! Photo: Doz777, pixabay.com

Chapter Seven

No More Bad Dogs!

Dogs don't want to go bad. They need you to teach them good dog behaviour.

When your dog barks, or has an accident on the rug, or rips up the couch cushions or makes some other mess, are they being 'bad' on purpose?

Yes...and no. There is a reason for this behaviour that people don't like. But to dogs, they're just doing what comes naturally to them.

Some will get into the kitchen garbage, spreading it all over the floor, if you don't put a tight lid on the garbage container that they can't open.

Some will make a huge barking racket when people come to visit.

Some could trash your house when you're not home. Or do other annoying things, like eat poo, dig up the garden and run away when you call them.

What to do about 'bad' dog behaviour

Some of these 'bad' behaviours are signs of a dog that just hasn't learned good manners yet. But others are more serious signs of a fearful and distressed dog. When you understand what your dog is telling you with his behaviour, you can work with him to solve the problem.

This takes time and effort, but you will have a happier dog. And you will be a happier dog owner.

For help with dog behaviour problems, ask the teacher at your puppy obedience training class to recommend a good dog behaviour trainer.

Remember, dogs want to be trained. They want to be good pets and have their owners happy with them. They just need to be shown better habits than what their dog brain is telling them to do right now.

Dogs left alone too much can get into trouble because they're bored.

What can you do about pet stains?

Pets that are very stressed, sick, very young or very old might leave pet stains on your bed, furniture, cushions, rugs or their bed.

If normal washing with soap and warm water doesn't get rid of the stains, use pet stain remover. Buy it online or at pet stores. It works when you follow the instructions on the bottle.

Pets will keep peeing (weeing) in the same spot unless you clean it completely with vinegar and water, or else with pet stain remover.

What about digging in the garden?

Some dogs just have to dig! Show them where they are allowed to dig and what part of the garden is off limits for digging (or using as a toilet).

How do you stop chewing?

Dogs need to chew, especially when their adult teeth are coming in. Buy rubber chew toys – the type that you can put treats inside. Dogs will get hours of fun out of chewing on these.

Dogs who chew, or tear up the house, or bark a lot, or howl are bored and lonely. They need more playtime with you and more exercise.

For a dog, getting plenty of outdoor exercise is so important! Dogs go bonkers without it. Often, bad dog behaviour vanishes when a dog gets lots of fresh air and times to run at the dog park.

Dogs also love outdoor games like catch-the-frisbee. You could use dog treats to set up a hunt-the-treat game for them, with treats hidden around your yard, or one part of the dog park.

How should you discipline your puppy or dog?

Losing your temper with your dog doesn't work. Shouting at her, or hitting, shaking or slapping will just make them not like you. It won't change their behaviour. Also, doing any of these things is cruel.

The name for being cruel to animals is "animal abuse."

Do this instead. Call their name or clap your hands loudly to get their attention. Then show them something better to do right now. Use praise and treats to get the behaviour you want.

It's also important to be consistent (say this word like this: con-sis-tent). Consistent means having a routine and always doing things the same way.

You can't play roughly with your puppy or dog one day, then be angry the next day when your dog wants to play rough some more and she nips you. Dogs, like people, like to know what to expect. It makes them a little bit crazy when the rules are always changing. This is true for people, too.

With puppies, the thing to do is always reward good behaviour. Mostly ignore what you don't want them to do unless it is seriously bad behaviour.

Don't get excited and angry and start shouting. Dogs don't understand this. It just makes them over-excited and anxious or afraid.

When a dog is over-excited, barking and jumping up, pretend you are a tree. Look down to the ground, not at the dog. They will immediately stop and look at you.

If your dog does this when your friends come to visit, tell them to be a tree so your dog will calm down and listen to you. Praise your dog when he sits and looks up at you. He will learn that even when people come to the door, he doesn't need to bark. He can greet your guests politely.

Two dogs playing at the beach.

Should you get two dogs so they have a companion?

Dogs are pack animals, used to living in groups. They worry when they're on their own.

It is better for dogs not to be home alone for more than short amounts of time. One solution is to get two puppies, or two dogs that are already friends.

<u>Chapter Eight</u>

What To Name Your New Pet Puppy

This is a Border Collie.

It's fun to choose a name for your new pet! But what name will you choose?

If you adopt a puppy, he or she probably won't already have a name. An adult dog might already have a name, but adult dogs can learn to answer to a new name if you really don't like their 'old' name.

A puppy or a dog can learn their name or new name in a few days.

Here's how to do it:

1. Carry dog treats in your pocket.

2. Call out your dog's name and immediately give her a treat.

3. She will quickly learn that the word that is her name means a treat is coming and look at you.

The most popular names for dogs are Maggie and Molly for females and Max and Jake for males.

Some other 'people' names for dogs are Sammy, Kelly, Timmie and Pat.

Or you could choose a name because of the colour of your dog's coat like Blackie, Midnight, Shadow or Peaches.

You could give your dog a 'hero' name, like Spike, Caesar, Nero, Duke, Prince or Princess.

Or the name of a famous dog, like Lassie, Rinty or Benji.

Or choose a quirky name, like Fender, Widget or Gromit.

Remember, you and your dog are going to be best friends for a long time.

Choose a name you really like. Your dog doesn't care what it is, just as long as you never forget it!

A Few Final Words

Well here we are. You've come to the last page and now we're asking you for a kind favour.

Would you be willing to submit an honest review about this book and your experience reading it? You might need an adult to help you do this.

Your review could help someone else decide to give it a try.

Of course, we hope for a positive review, but most important is an honest one.

So, if you could take a few moments to help us and anyone who might be considering reading this book, thanks so much.

And warm best wishes,

Jackie, Wayne and Jesse

The team at CrimsonHillBooks.com

Crimson Hill
Books

More Fun Books For Kids Who Love Pets!

Best Pets for Kids series:

I Want A Leopard Gecko

I Want A Bearded Dragon

I Want A Puppy

I Want A Kitten

Fun Animal Facts for Kids series:

Fun Dog Facts For Kids 9-12

Fun Cat Facts For Kids 9-12

Fun Leopard Gecko and Bearded Dragon Facts For Kids 9-12

Fun Reptile Facts For Kids 9-12

Fun Pets for Kids series:

Small Fun Pets: Beginning Pets For Kids 9-12

Top 10 Fun Pets for Kids 9-12

Find them all at:
www.CrimsonHillBooks.com

Lightning Source UK Ltd.
Milton Keynes UK
UKHW050654021222
413206UK00001B/6